Milly's Wheels

Two Girls and a Reading Corner
www.twogirlsandareadingcorner.com

MILLY'S WHEELS
TWO GIRLS AND A READING CORNER
Copyright ©2021 LUCY MALKANI
ISBN: 978-1-952879-12-8

Cover Art and Illustrations by VAN ANDREWS
Edited by MELANIE LOPATA

This is a work of fiction. All rights reserved. Any memories shared in this book are from the author's perspective. Certain names may have been changed to protect those involved. Any trademarks, service marks, product names, or named features are assumed to be the property of their respective owners and are used only for reference. There is no implied endorsement if any of these terms are used. Except for review purposes, the reproduction of this book in whole or part, electronically or mechanically, constitutes a copyright violation.

For permission requests, please email
twogirlsandareadingcorner@gmail.com
Place "Request for Permissions" in the subject line or contact:
Two Girls and a Reading Corner
PO Box 2404, Madison, AL 35758

To my nephew, Ethan, and niece, Ruby who kept asking for Milly stories and used to take wonderful care of Milly, my cousin, Caleb for his veterinarian advice and to all the sweet Fur babies who helped inspire me to write about my precious Milly.

Milly, a black and brown puppy, joyfully pricked her ears up when she heard her mom bark, "Milly, we're going camping at the lake this weekend." Milly was so excited that she started scooting in circles. Milly scooted because she couldn't use her back legs, but that didn't stop her from doing what she loved, and camping was one of the things she loved best.

She wanted to do something different this time, though.

She would turn her chariot, which was a two-wheeled cart that helped support her back legs, into a submarine that would help her dive down into the depths of the lake.

Milly was concerned that there might be monsters in the lake and wanted to be prepared in case she saw one, so she decided to build bubble blasters that would attach to her submarine.

She went to the hardware store with her mom where she bought purple lasers, green propellers, a breathing tube, and a bright blue periscope. She went home and busily worked on fixing up her new and improved chariot.

When Milly went to bed that night, she could hardly sleep as she was very excited about going to the lake!

She woke up to see the sun shining through her window.

She heard her dad yip, "The car is packed and we're ready to leave!"

Milly sat in her car seat, her eyes shining with excitement.

When they arrived at the lake, Milly's mom took her out of her seat and gently put her on the ground. Milly started scooting to the water as fast as she could move. Her mom saw her and barked for Milly to wait for her chariot.

Milly ran back and stepped into her cart and then zoomed into the water. She was shaking with excitement, not wanting to wait to see if her magic chariot would become a submarine. Using her nose, she pushed the button to submerge and she sank to the sandy bottom of the lake. It worked!

Milly looked around and began driving her submarine so she could explore the bottom of the lake. She saw little silver minnows, different colored rocks, and blue shells. She was thrilled by the beauty of it all. Suddenly, a huge, black shadow appeared in front of her! She squealed with excitement and swam after the shadow.
RRRRRRRRRRRRRTTTTTTTTTTTWWWWWWWWW whirred her little submarine.

The shadow turned around. It was a gigantic yellow and green sea monster with brown and purple spots! It saw Milly and it swam towards her.

Milly's eyes were wide with fright until she remembered her bubble blasters!

She pulled the lever by her seat, and out popped two bubble blasters on the sides of her submarine. She thought *HERE I GO!* as she pushed the button, and millions of bubbles blew out of her blasters.

The sea monster saw the bubbles and started chasing them, as they were a lot more interesting than a tiny pink and blue submarine. Milly was thrilled that her invention had worked.

That night after a yummy chicken dinner and s'mores by the campfire with her mom and dad, she told her parents about her adventure.

It was time to go back home. Milly sat in her car seat thinking of the fun time she had with her bubble submarine. She couldn't wait to see what would happen on her next adventure with her magic chariot!

Acknowledgments

I'd like to thank my wonderful publisher, Mandy Leigh, for giving me this opportunity and for being very helpful and kind throughout the whole process. I'm blessed to have her and her husband who brought Milly to life with his gorgeous illustrations. I'd also like to thank my sister, Anna, and my husband for pushing me to send off my story to get published. Thank you wonderful readers for your support in buying my book.

About the Author

After a grand time of teaching third grade for seven years and kindergarten for 4 years, Lucy Malkani fulfilled her other childhood dream of being a children's author. In her free time, she loves to spend time with her nieces and nephews, train her cat, Pumpkin, spend time with her husband, read, write, and hike. She resides in El Paso, Texas, where she has lived for eight years.

About the Illustrator

Van Andrews was born in Buffalo, New York and raised in Florida. He now resides in Madison, Al. Van has enjoyed drawing at a young age from abstract art to superheroes. His senior year in high school, he took World Literature and it opened the realm of writing for him. He got lost within the ink as it fell to paper and enjoyed creating a world of words. After graduating high school, he enlisted in the Marine Corps and served 4 years as an Aviation Ordnance Systems Technician. Van is married to his wonderful wife and they have 4 children together: Sadie, Tyler, Lulee and Brynlea...The 3 being his bonus daughters.

Two Girls and a Reading Corner

P.O. Box 2404

Madison, AL 35758

Made in the USA
Middletown, DE
18 June 2023